CONTENTS

ANIMAL KINGDOM

DAVID BURNIE, CLAIRE LLEWELLYN AND MIRANDA SMITH

KINGFISHER

KINGFISHER

First published 2016 by Kingfisher
an imprint of Macmillan Children's Books
20 New Wharf Road, London N1 9RR
Associated companies throughout the world
www.panmacmillan.com

Copyright © Macmillan Publishers International Ltd 2016

ISBN 978-0-7534-3932-6

Consultant: David Burnie
Illustrations by: Polygone Studio, Barry Croucher, Steve Weston,
Gary Hanna, Peter Bull Art Studio

Printed in China
9 8 7 6 5 4 3 2 1
1TR/0216/UTD/WKT/128MA

A CIP catalogue record for this book is available from the British Library.

Note to readers: The website addresses listed in this book are correct at the time of publishing.
However, due to the ever-changing nature of the internet, website addresses and content can change.
Websites can contain links that are unsuitable for children. The publisher cannot be held responsible for
changes in website addresses or content, or for information obtained through third-party websites.
We strongly advise that internet searches should be supervised by an adult.

INVESTIGATE ICONS:

 Book to read

 Place to visit

 Website to visit

The Publisher would like to thank the following for permission to reproduce their material.
(t = top, b = bottom, c = centre, r = right, l = left):
Cover tl Shutterstock/James Arup; tc Shutterstock/Sari ONeal; tr Shutterstock/aaltair; c Shutterstock/Serguei Koultchitskii; br Shutterstock/tawan, Shutterstock/JY Loke; spine iStock/strandwolf;
Back cover cl iStock/GlobalP; bc iStock/cynoclub; cr iStock/impalastock; bcr iStock/komodo-adv; Pages 1 iStock/GlobalP; 3–4 iStock/JurgaR; 5 iStock/BenGoode; 6tl Corbis/Manfred Danegger;
6tr Shutterstock/Vladimir Melnik; 6cl Shutterstock/Mogens Trolle; 6c Shutterstock/Joy Brown; 6cr FLPA/Hugh Lansdown; 6br Shutterstock/Eric Isselee; 6–7t Naturepl/Brendon Cole; 6–7b Shutterstock/
Susan Flashman; 7tr Roger Ingle/Flora & Fauna International; 7c Shutterstock/Sharon Morris; 7r Shutterstock/Milena; 7bl Ardea/John Daniels; 7br Naturepl/Anup Shah; 8tl iStock/f9photos;
8tr Shutterstock/Matt Gibson; 8cl Dreamstime/Isselee; 8cr Shutterstock/AngeloDeVal; 8bl iStock/frentusha; 9 iStock/Enjoylife2; 10–11 Yvan Muenier; 10bl FLPA/Frank Stober; 11tl FLPA/Minden/
Michael Durham; 11tr Alamy/David Hosking; 12–13 Naturepl/T.J.Rich; 12lc Getty/NGS; 13tr Seapics/Michael S. Nolan; 13b Peter Bull; 14lc NHPA; 14–15 NHPA/Photoshot; 15t Getty/Gallo
Images-Londolozi Productions; 15c NHPA/Daryl Balfour; 15bl Naturepl/Martin Dohrn; 15br Getty/Steve Bloom; 16tr FLPA/Jurgen & Christine Sohns; 16cl Shutterstock/Patsy Michaud;
16b Shutterstock/H. Damke; 19tl Shutterstock/mlorenz; 19tr Superstock/Age fotostock; 20tl Naturepl/Dan Burton; 20tr SPL/Paul Gunning; 20c Shutterstock/MikeE; 21tl Naturepl/John Downer;
21bl Alamy/blickwinkel; 21tr Photoshot/Nigel J Dennis/NHPA; 21cr Photoshot/Nigel J Dennis/NHPA; 22tr Shutterstock/Larsek; 22cl Alamy/Paul Maguire; 22–23 Shutterstock/Gail Johnson; 23tl FLPA/
Michio Hoshino/Minden; 23tr FLPA/Imagebroker; 23br Alamy/Accent Alaska.com; 24tr SPL/Andrew Syred; 24c Getty/OSF; 24bl Alamy/WorldFoto; 24–25 Shutterstock/Pichugin Dmitry; 25cl SPL/
Andrew Syred; 25cr Alamy/age fotostock; 25br Getty/Joe McDonald; 26tl iStock/pailoolom; 26tr Shutterstock/Maggy Meyer; 26cl Shutterstock/DarZel; 26cr iStock/GlobalP; 26b iStock/chuvipro;
27 iStock/ajsn; 28tl Alamy/William Leaman; 28br Photoshot/Woodfall Wild Images; 28–29 Corbis/DLILLC; 29tl Naturepl/David Pike; 29tr Naturepl/David Pike; 29br Getty/NGS/Tim Laman; 30l Nicky
Studdart; 30tr Naturepl/Richard du Toit; 30br Ardea/Dominic Usher; 31tr Nicky Studdart; 31bl Shutterstock/Matin Fowler; 31br Photoshot/NHPA; 32–33 Polygone Studios; 32l Shutterstock/Volt
Collection; 32tr Alamy/blickwinkel; 33t FLPA/Andrew Forsyth; 34tr Peter Bull; 34bl Naturepl/Rolf Nussbaumer; 34–35 Shutterstock/Mark Medcalf; 35tl FLPA/Minden/Tim Fitzharris; 35tr Naturepl/
Charlie Hamilton James; 35cr Naturepl/Charlie Hamilton James; 35br Shutterstock/siete_vidas; 35bl Shutterstock/apiguide; 35bc Naturepl/Bernard Castelein; 35br Shutterstock/siete_vidas;
36tl Shutterstock/Mark Medcalf; 36tr iStock/Mr_Jamsey; 36cl iStock/MikeLane45; 36cr iStock/PrinPrince; 36bl iStock/otto_pro; 37 iStock/JanelleLugge; 38–39 Polygone Studios; 39rc Alamy/Scott
Camazine; 39b Natural Sciences Image Lib (NSIL) New Zealand; 40br Seapics; 41 Getty/Digital Vision; 41cr Corbis/JoeMcDonald; 41c Getty/Visuals Unlimited/Joe McDonald; 42tl Alamy/
42tr Nature PL/Daniel Gomez; 42bl PA/AP; 42–43 c & l SPL/Paul Whitten; 44 Ardea/Kathie Atkinson; 45tr FLPA/Minden Pictures; 45cr FLPA/Minden Pictures; 45b FLPA/Minden Pictures;
46tl Naturepl/Tim Macmillan/John Downer Productions; 46b Getty/DEA / C.DANI / I.JESKE; 46rt Getty Images; 46br Naturepl/Barry Mansell; 47tl Photoshot/NHPA; 47tr FLPA/Jurgen & Christine
Sohns; 47c Shutterstock/Mark Bridger; 47bl Photoshot/NHPA; 48–49t Corbis/Joe McDonald; 48b Shutterstock/Tomas Hilger; 49tr Naturepl/Jane Burton; 49b Shutterstock/Dirck Ercken; 50tl Getty/
50tl FLPA/Minden Pictures; 50tr FLPA/Minden Pictures; 50br FLPA; 51tr Corbis/Wolfgang Kaehler; 51b NHPA/Daniel Heuclin; 52tr Nature PL/Anup Shah; 52 FLPA/Fritz Polking; 54–55 Yvan Muenier;
55tr FLPA/Christian Kapteyn; 55bl Photoshot/NHPA/Anthony Bannister; 56tl iStock/Anna Omelchenko; 56tr Shutterstock/orlandin; 56cl iStock/amwu; 56cr Shutterstock/Aleksy Stemmer;
56bl Dreamstime/Michalnapartowicz; 57 iStock/VitalyEdush; 58–59 Seapics/Masa Ushioda; 58c Seapics/Masa Ushioda; 58b Seapics/David B. Fleetham; 59c Peter Bull; 59tc Naturepl/Georgette
Douwma; 59tr Shutterstock; 59r FLPA/R. Dirscherl; 59b Seapics/Edward G. Lines; 60tl Shutterstock/Wolfgang Amri; 60bl Shutterstock/Luis Chavier; 60c Shutterstock/ivvv1975; 60cr Shutterstock/Olga
Khoroshunova; 60br Shutterstock/Rui Gomes; 60–61 Shutterstock/John A. Anderson; 61cl Alamy/David Fleetham; 61cr Shutterstock/Milena Katzer; 61b Shutterstock/Rich Carey; 63tl SPL/Peter
Scoones; 63b Imagequest Marine; 64tr Getty/Berndt Fischer; 64bl Ardea/Mike Watson; 65t Corbis/Gerolf Kalt; 66tl iStock/VitalyEdush; 66tr Dreamstime/Hbh; 66cl iStock/think4photop; 66cr iStock/
DavidByronKeener; 66bl Dreamstime/Marty Wakat; 67 iStock/Spydr; 68–69 Naturepl/Doug Perrine; 68tl Naturepl/Jose B. Ruiz; 69cr SPL/Laguna Design; 69b Corbis/Dan Guravich; 70cl FLPA/Moden/
Michael & Patricia Fogden; 70b Photoshot/NHPA; 70r Shutterstock; 71t Naturepl/Hans Christoph Kappel; 71c Shutterstock; 71b Getty/Paul Zahl; 72tr & c Naturepl/Martin Dohrn; 73 tl & tc FLPA/
Minden Pictures; 74c FLPA/Minden Pictures; 75 Animals/Animals/Roger de la Harpe; 74–75 Corbis/Wayne Lynch/All Canada Photos; 76tl Dreamstime/Dannyphoto80; 76tr Shutterstock/juk astrasat;
76cl Dreamstime/Budda; 76cr Dreamstime/Andrey Pavlov; 76bl Dreamstime/Costasz; 78tl Shutterstock/reptiles4all; 80tl Shutterstock/juk astrasat.

A WORLD
OF ANIMALS

Birds

These vertebrates walk on two feet, are warm-blooded and lay eggs. They rule the skies, having evolved feathers, wings and a lightweight skeleton for flight. Birds have beaks and range from meat-eating birds of prey, such as a barn owl (above), to hummingbirds that sip nectar from flowers.

Reptiles

Reptiles are cold-blooded vertebrates with tough, scaly skin. They breathe air, and live on land and in water. Most reptiles lay eggs, but some give birth to live young. Their body shapes vary greatly, from long, legless cobras (above) to shell-covered turtles.

ANIMALS EVERYWHERE

Fish

Covered with scales, these vertebrates are able to move easily through the water they live in, manoeuvring their streamlined body with their fins. They take oxygen from the water using gills. Most fish lay eggs, but some, such as the great white shark (right), give birth to live young.

Animals inhabit every nook and cranny on Earth. Some are vertebrates (animals with backbones), but the vast majority are invertebrates (animals with no backbone). Most animals, including invertebrates and reptiles, are cold-blooded, which means that their body temperature is determined by their surroundings. Warm-blooded birds and mammals are able to make and maintain their own body heat. All animals get the energy they need from the food they eat.

 Nearly two million species of animals have been identified, and 97 per cent of them are invertebrates.

Invertebrates

These animals do not have a backbone or an internal skeleton made of bone. They are an incredibly large and varied group. Some, such as jellyfish (below), have soft bodies. Others, such as insects and molluscs, have hard outer cases or shells.

Mammals

Although most mammals live on land, some fly and swim. All of these vertebrates, except for monotremes, give birth to live young that feed on milk produced by the female. Mammals range in size from the tiny bumblebee bat to the African elephant (left).

Amphibians

Most of these cold-blooded vertebrates start life in water, as larvae that breathe using gills. As they grow, the larvae change shape into adults that breathe using lungs, like this tree frog (right).

INVESTIGATE

Find out what the experts know about animals, and explore the animal kingdom by checking out safari parks, museums, books and websites.

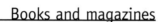

Zoos and safari parks

Visit a zoo or safari park for a close-up view of all kinds of animals, and to find out about conservation measures to protect animals in the wild.

 The Truth about the Most Dangerous Creatures on Earth by Nicola Davies (Walker)

 Africa Alive! Whites Lane, Kessingland, Lowestoft, Suffolk NR33 7TF

www.wellingtonzoo.com

The Sumatran tiger of Indonesia is a critically endangered species.

The koala is a marsupial, native to Australia.

Books and magazines

To find out more about the animal kingdom and to see some amazing photographs, check out some of the many animal information books and wildlife magazines.

 Navigators: Killer Creatures by Claire Llewellyn (Kingfisher)

 Wildlife Photographer of the Year exhibition, Natural History Museum, Cromwell Road, London SW7 5BD

 www.discoverwildlife.com

This trap-door spider is about to attack.

Museums and exhibitions

Many museums, local, national and online, stage special exhibitions and have interactive displays that provide expert information to visitors about all kinds of animals.

Stinging anemones provide clownfish with protection from predators.

 World's Deadliest Animals by Matt Roper (Summersdale)

 National Museum of Scotland, Chambers Street, Edinburgh EH1 1JF

 http://issuu.com/manchestermuseum/docs/_the_manchester_museum_amazingfacts

Documentaries and movies

Wildlife documentaries on television or movies at the cinema, on DVD and online give fascinating and beautifully filmed insights into the animal kingdom.

 Big Cat Diary: Cheetah by Jonathan Scott and Angela Scott (Collins)

 IMAX 3D cinema, Science Museum, Exhibition Road, London SW7 2DD

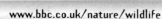 www.bbc.co.uk/nature/wildlife

MAMMALS

FINDING FOOD

To keep warm, to grow and to give their bodies energy, mammals need to eat. The smaller the mammals, the quicker they lose body heat, so it is important to eat frequently – in the case of shrews, almost all day long. Carnivores scavenge upon or hunt other animals, herbivores eat plants, and omnivores eat both plants and animals. And sometimes, because of weather or time of year, food can be hard to find.

> "All animals are equal, but some animals are more equal than others."
>
> **George Orwell (1903–1950)**
> *British author, from his novel* Animal Farm *(1945)*

A nose for ants

The giant anteater of South and Central America has an acute sense of smell, which leads it to a termite mound or ant nest. It breaks into the sandy walls of the mound with sharp claws, making a hole that is large enough for its long, narrow snout and tongue. The anteater may lap up as many as 35,000 termites and ants a day from several mounds.

Hunting on the wing

A bat finds its prey by using echolocation to decide its shape, size, distance and direction of travel. The mammal emits high-pitched sounds that bounce as echoes off objects. The bat listens to the echoes, and homes in on moths and other prey.

Claws are tucked under to protect them while walking.

Treetop feeders

The tallest of all the animals that live on land, the giraffe has evolved to feed at a level that is out of reach of other herbivores. Its favourite food on the grasslands of Africa is the thorny acacia tree. The giraffe's long neck, which is made up of seven elongated vertebrae, allows it to browse the topmost branches.

> The smallest mammal in the world is the Savi's pygmy shrew, which is 6cm long from nose to tip of tail.

⊖ TINY ANIMAL, BIG APPETITE

Shrews are aggressive hunters that forage for anything, from seeds and spiders to small mammals and birds. They have a high metabolism and need to eat 80–90 per cent of their own body weight each day. Most have poor eyesight and locate prey by smell. Like bats, whales, dolphins and some birds, certain shrew species give ultrasonic squeaks, using echolocation to target prey.

A common shrew eats a worm. This tiny mammal is most often found in grassland and woodland.

A termite mound will be visited again and again.

The second and third fingers have long, powerful claws, used mainly for digging and defence.

Its sticky tongue can reach up to 60cm inside the mound.

STORAGE AND DIGESTION

Many mammals need to store food, either in a safe place or inside their own bodies, because of the extreme conditions of their habitats. In all cases, the food needs to be broken down before the nutrients can be absorbed. The majority of mammals bite and chew food before digesting, while others, such as humpback whales, swallow their food whole.

RUMINANT - *hoofed mammal with a specialized digestive system, and two stomachs*

Hoarding food

The African leopard is a very strong animal. It has a large head on muscular shoulders and can weigh up to 90kg. This strong, agile meat-eater is capable of climbing a 15m-high tree with a large, dead springbok as heavy as itself in its mouth. It drags its prey there to keep it safe from scavenging lions and hyenas.

The camel's hump
Camels are well adapted to living in areas of the world where food is sometimes scarce. Their humps store fat, a fuel for their bodies to use when needed.

A camel can go with little or no food or water for up to seven days.

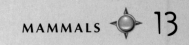

Bubble nets can be up to 30m in diameter.

Humpback whales form nets of bubbles around shoals of fish and krill. The whales then surface through the shoal with their mouths open, swallowing their prey.

Hairy baleen plates filter the fish and krill out of the seawater.

www.alaskawhalefoundation.org

Whale restaurant

In their search for food, many humpback whales visit the cold Pacific waters off the coast of Alaska. They spend several months at this rich feeding-ground, eating as much as they can. They have to put on enough weight to be able to live off their fat reserves for the rest of the year.

The leopard hunts at night and often suffocates prey by clamping its jaws over the animal's nose

⊖ INSIDE A RUMINANT'S STOMACH

Although plants, and particularly grasses, are often easy to find, they are very hard to digest. Many herbivores have bacteria inside their bodies that help release nutrients from tough plant matter. Ruminants such as buffaloes have four chambers in their first stomach. The largest, the rumen, contains millions of these bacteria.

rumen

reticulum

omasum

abomasum

ATTACK AND DEFENCE

DEFENCE – *protection of someone or something from attack*

Mammals are successful because they are very adaptable. Some predators, such as lions, work together to take down prey, while others, including tigers, are lone hunters. Camouflage (blending into the background) is a great defence against predators. Herds provide protection for weaker members – musk oxen form defensive rings round their young when threatened.

"The scientific name of an animal that doesn't either run from or fight its enemies is lunch."

Michael Friedman (born 1960)
American poet

Best defence
When a wolf snarls, it is a terrifying sight – enough to make most attackers take to their heels. By displaying their teeth in this way, wolves have found a very effective method of defence.

Distracting patterns
The black and white markings on a zebra are unique to that individual animal. When a herd of zebra is moving together it is hard for a predator, such as a crocodile, to make out where one animal ends and another begins. This patterning is called disruptive coloration, and it is a superb defence.

 ❯ Green algae growing in the fur of sloths help to camouflage them in the rainforest.

⊖ ARMOURED BALL

When threatened, an armadillo – Spanish for 'little armoured one' – rolls up into a ball. Its soft underside is protected by the bony, skin-covered armour on the top of its body and tail. Pangolins protect themselves in a similar fashion, their upper bodies covered by overlapping scales. The hedgehog, by contrast, has spines all over its back and sides, and forms a prickly ball.

three-banded armadillo

hinged back allows flexibility

defensive ball is impenetrable

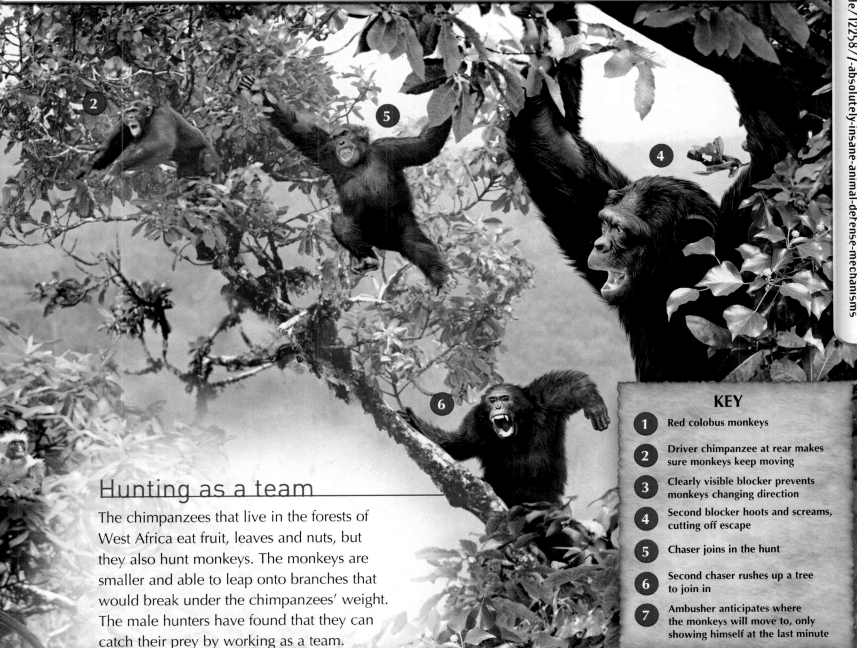

Hunting as a team

The chimpanzees that live in the forests of West Africa eat fruit, leaves and nuts, but they also hunt monkeys. The monkeys are smaller and able to leap onto branches that would break under the chimpanzees' weight. The male hunters have found that they can catch their prey by working as a team.

KEY

1 Red colobus monkeys

2 Driver chimpanzee at rear makes sure monkeys keep moving

3 Clearly visible blocker prevents monkeys changing direction

4 Second blocker hoots and screams, cutting off escape

5 Chaser joins in the hunt

6 Second chaser rushes up a tree to join in

7 Ambusher anticipates where the monkeys will move to, only showing himself at the last minute

STRENGTH IN NUMBERS

In many parts of the world, rodents outnumber all other mammals put together. There are more than 2,000 kinds, living almost everywhere on land, as well as in rivers, streams and ponds. Some are large, but most are small, fast-moving animals that try to keep out of sight. Rodents have sharp front teeth, and they gnaw through plants and seeds. Small rodents – such as mice and voles – breed at an amazing rate, but predators usually keep their numbers under control.

Productive parents
A female house mouse can have up to 80 babies a year. Blind and helpless at birth, her young grow up fast. By the age of ten weeks, they are fully mature and ready to have their own families.

golden-mantled ground squirrel

Cheeky
Like many small rodents, this ground squirrel from North America has flexible cheek pouches, which work like shopping bags. It fills its pouches with seeds, and then scampers to its burrow to store them underground.

Beavers gnaw through trees up to 25cm across, using their incisor teeth. These flat-bladed teeth have a self-sharpening front edge and long roots that curve towards the back of the jaws.

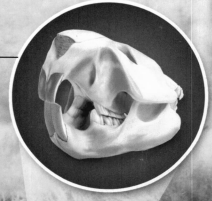

North America beaver dam

Beaver fur is waterproofed by a strongly scented natural oil, produced in glands near the tail

⊖ GIANT RODENTS

Capybaras are the world's largest rodents. Looking like giant guinea pigs, they live in marshy places in South America, where they feed on waterside plants. Adult males measure up to 1.3m long, and can weigh as much as an adult man. Capybaras are related to guinea pigs, so the resemblance is not just skin-deep. But a capybara is specially adapted for swimming, with slightly webbed feet, and eyes and nostrils high up on its head.

Capybaras have barrel-shaped bodies and short legs.

> The largest-known beaver dam, in Canada, is 850m long. It was found using satellite pictures in 2010.

"In time, a mouse will gnaw
through a cable."

Dutch and German proverb

The lodge is a hollow
mound of branches,
with concealed entrances
below the waterline.

Master builders

Many animals build their own homes, but beavers are
the only mammals that make dams across streams and
rivers. It is an immense task, and they do it to protect
their homes, or lodges, and to store winter food. To make
a dam, beavers cut down waterside trees and skilfully
float them into place. The dam is then sealed with mud
and clay. Large dams are made by several generations
of beavers, and can be more than 50 years old.

Small eyes, positioned high
on the head, are covered
by see-through
membranes
when diving.

Beavers chew
through hard, old
wood – as well as
the soft saplings that
they eat – using
their powerful
jaw muscles.

www.onekind.org/be_inspired/animals_a_z/beaver/

WEANING – the change from mother's milk to a more grown-up diet

Sharp vision picks up the slightest sign of movement against the snow.

Ears swivel back and forth to pick up sounds – a feature shared by dogs, which are descended from wolves.

HUNTING IN A PACK

Instead of hunting alone, grey wolves often live and hunt in packs. It is an efficient way of life, because it lets wolves prey on animals that are too big and too strong for them to tackle on their own. A pack usually contains up to 12 adult wolves, led by a dominant – or 'alpha' – pair. The dominant pair mate for life and produce all the pack's young. When they are too old to breed, younger members of the pack take their place.

Closing in

After a long chase through Canada's wintry landscape, a pack of wolves closes in on a moose. Moose are the world's largest deer – a big adult male can weigh more than 500kg, which is over ten times as much as an average Arctic wolf. But numbers and stamina count. Guided by their keen senses, the wolves move in to make the kill.

 > Despite their bad reputation, wolves have hardly ever been known to attack people.

Call of the wild

Wolf packs stake out a territory so that they have enough space to hunt. They claim territory by marking it with scent, and by howling. Their eerie chorus keeps neighbouring packs away.

Despite its powerful body, the moose is not a good fighter. Its antlers are for show, rather than for attack.

Something for everyone

After most hunts, all the wolves usually eat some part of the kill. Meat is carried back to the den for cubs that are being weaned. In good times, wolves bury half-eaten food, consuming it weeks or even months later.

⊖ SNAP ATTACK

wolves surround the moose

moose's hindquarters vulnerable to attack

moose forced to stand its ground

The end of the hunt comes when the wolves surround the moose, cutting off its escape route. With the moose in snapping range, they dart forwards to bite its unprotected underside, or grip its muzzle tightly in their jaws. The moose spins around to fend off the attacks, but finally falls as the pack moves in.

SELF-DEFENCE

At the first sign of trouble, most mammals try to make an emergency escape. Some run, while others swim or fly, but a small number (mostly plant-eaters) use special defences to hold their ground. They include pangolins, which have built-in armour plating, and also porcupines, which are protected by hundreds of hollow quills, which are long, stiff and very sharp. When fully raised, they can keep an adult lion at bay.

An African porcupine's quills have backward-facing barbs that catch on skin and make them hard to pull out.

> An African porcupine's quills can be 30cm long. American porcupines have shorter and softer quills.

Two against one

With its back facing danger, an African porcupine tries to fend off two hungry lions. The lions are intent on flipping it over, so they can reach its furry underside. Each time they move closer, the porcupine rattles its quills and reverses. The quills can detach easily, embedding themselves in a lion's skin.

Chemical defences

Performing a handstand, this skunk can squirt an evil-smelling fluid from glands beneath its tail. The fluid contains a high concentration of sulphur – the same substance that gives burning rubber its stomach-churning reek.

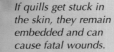

If quills get stuck in the skin, they remain embedded and can cause fatal wounds.

Like most cats, lions can extend and retract their claws. This makes sure they are always sharp.

⊖ ARMOUR PLATING

Millions of years ago, giant, armoured mammals roamed the Earth. Some were as big as cars. These giants eventually died out, but armoured mammals still exist today – including armadillos, which are covered in bony plates, and pangolins, which have overlapping scales. Some kinds roll up to protect soft body parts inside.

Pangolin stops and tucks in its head when threatened.

Legs disappear beneath the pangolin's sharp-edged scales.

Tail curls up, hiding the legs and head, and completing the ball.

FOLLOW THE LEADER

HERD INSTINCT – *an instinct that makes mammals stay together*

Hoofed mammals often spend their lives in herds. By staying together, they have a better chance of spotting danger, and less chance of being singled out and attacked. Wildebeest and caribou form herds hundreds of thousands strong, but in the past, some antelope herds contained ten million animals, and were more than 100 kilometres long. Today, many farm animals live in herds, which makes them easy to control.

Wildebeest have curved, hollow horns. During the breeding season, males sometimes use them to ram their rivals.

Each front hoof has a gland that leaves a trail of scent. Wildebeest can use the scent to find their way back to the herd.

Life on the move

Surrounded by clouds of dust, common wildebeest migrate across Africa's Serengeti plain. Every year, they travel up to 2,500km, letting them make the most of the seasonal rains. Wildebeest spend the dry season in wooded grassland, until instinct tells them that it is time to move. Gathering in immense lines, they stream across the landscape, giving birth to their calves on the way. By the time the wet season comes, the wildebeest arrive in lush grassland where they feast on the annual burst of food.

> Most wildebeest give birth in a three-week 'slot', so their young are almost exactly the same age as each other.

Swimming herds

In the Canadian Arctic, caribou spend winter in forests, and summer in the open tundra. Their journey can be up to 5,000km long – a record for a land mammal. On the way, they often have to swim across sea inlets and lakes.

Time out

Wildebeest give birth in the open and their young soon follow the herd. Most deer and gazelles are different. This baby deer, or fawn, was born in thick undergrowth. It will stay hidden until it is several weeks old.

Wildebeest travel together, or in mixed herds with other mammals such as gazelles and zebras.

http://video.nationalgeographic.com/video/wildebeest_migration

Defensive circle

Musk oxen live in the far north of Canada, the USA and Greenland where the biggest danger comes from wolves. If a herd is threatened, the adults form a defensive circle, with their massive horns facing outwards and their young in the centre.

▽ INSULATION – *a body layer that helps to stop an animal becoming too warm or too cold*

SURVIVING EXTREMES

Mammals live in some of the hottest, coldest, highest and driest places on Earth. Unlike humans, they do not have special equipment or clothing, but they do have physical features that help them to survive. These include amazingly warm fur, thick layers of body fat and unusual body chemistry that lets them get all their water from their food.

Cells in the hump store fat – a substance that provides energy when food is hard to find.

Beating the heat

Like many small desert mammals, the long-eared jerboa digs burrows and avoids the daytime heat by feeding after dark. It eats seeds and insects, and survives on 'metabolic water' – water that it makes chemically from its food.

range: deserts of Central Asia, from Mongolia to China

High life

Vicuñas live at altitudes of up to 5,500m, where the oxygen in the air is extremely thin. Here, human hikers soon get tired, but vicuñas can run up steep slopes with ease. Their secret: special red blood cells that get the most oxygen from every breath.

range: Andes mountains, from Peru to Chile

 ▷ In the Arctic of northern Canada, some ground squirrels hibernate for nine months each year.

Double protection

Bactrian camels live deep in Central Asia, where it is hot in summer and freezing in winter, and dry nearly all the time. They store fat in their two humps, and they keep warm because of a long winter coat, which falls off in large patches during spring.

range: deserts of Central Asia, from Mongolia to China

A camel's undercoat is made of fine hairs that trap air, creating an insulating layer that keeps its body warm.

Winter wrap

The Arctic fox is one of the world's most cold-proof mammals, thanks to its exceptionally thick winter fur. It can survive in temperatures as low as –50°C, using its bushy tail to protect its feet and face from the icy wind. In spring, its white winter coat is replaced by a much thinner one, coloured brownish-grey.

range: High Arctic, in North America, Europe and Asia

⊖ HIBERNATION

Instead of battling through the winter, some mammals hibernate. They look as though they are sleeping, but their bodies turn cold, and their hearts beat only a few times a minute. Like machines on standby, they need only a small amount of energy to stay alive. Rodents often hibernate in burrows, while bats may choose caves or abandoned mines.

little brown bats hibernating

INVESTIGATE

Find out more about mammals and their habitats by visiting safari parks, zoos and museums as well as checking out books and websites.

A leopard searches for prey on the Masai Mara Reserve, Kenya.

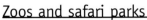

Zoos and safari parks

A trip to a safari park or zoo allows you to appreciate the beauty of mammals big and small at close range.

Wild Animal Atlas: Earth's Astonishing Animals and Where They Live (National Geographic)

Bristol Zoo Gardens, Clifton, Bristol BS8 3HA

www.woburnsafari.co.uk

The grey wolf howls to its pack across the wildernesses of Alaska.

Books and magazines

You can find expert information on mammals in books and magazines in a library and learn enough to become an expert yourself.

25 Most Deadly Animals in the World by IIC Wildlife (Amazon Kindle)

Subscribe to a magazine, such as Eco Kids Planet, www.ecokidsplanet.co.uk, to receive new information about animals every month.

www.animalfactguide.com

The oriental small-clawed otter, native to Southeast Asia, is the smallest otter in the world.

Museums and exhibitions

Visiting museums and exhibitions helps you to discover more about where mammals live and how they survive in the wild.

The Natural History Museum Book of Predators by Steve Parker (Natural History Museum)

Horniman Museum, 100 London Road, Forest Hill, London SE23 3PQ

www.kidsplanet.org/factsheets/map.html

Zebra parents mind their young in the Manyara region of Tanzania.

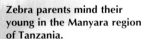

Documentaries and movies

Watching movies and documentaries is a really exciting way to see how mammals behave in their own environment.

The Life of Mammals (BBC Films)

Enter into any creature's natural habitat in your own home by searching for animal clips on the Internet.

www.bbc.co.uk/newsround/animals

BIRDS

DISPLAY – to attract a bird of the same species with colour, plumage or behaviour

Each individual adult male lazuli bunting has his own song.

The power of song

In spring, stimulated by the days getting longer, many birds sing vigorously and non-stop. It is the beginning of the mating season and they sing to defend their territory and attract a mate. Each species has its own song, and how the male sings will decide whether or not he is successful.

Each crane's wingspan is up to 2.5m.

ATTRACTING A MATE

Male birds use various techniques to attract a mate. Peacocks show off spectacular plumage, and red kites dive and swoop acrobatically in flight. Grebes 'rush' across water together, while woodpeckers drum rhythmically on hollow tree trunks. Bowerbirds build structures and Adélie penguins give pebbles as gifts. Many birds use song to find a mate – the tiny wren achieves an amazing 740 notes a minute and can be heard at a distance of 500 metres!

⊖ CHANGING SHAPE

Size is an important factor in the mating game. The male great frigate bird inflates a magnificent red chest pouch, while the tragopan of western China inflates its blue wattle. The male turkey's whole head changes colour when it becomes excited and its wattle also swells.

A male wild turkey swells its wattle in display.

> The Australian superb lyrebird mimics the mating calls of at least 20 other bird species.

Heads thrust back, two red-crowned cranes perform on the lek, or mating ground.

The cranes call, mirroring each other's movements.

The courtship dance includes a series of bows, head bobbing and leaps.

Males and females look alike.

Colourful display

There are 42 species of birds of paradise, and the males have some of the most colourful plumage in the world. In Papua New Guinea, natives have used the tail feathers of males as ceremonial decorations for centuries.

http://animals.nationalgeographic.com/animals/birds/bird-of-paradise

Dazzling dancers

Cranes have been adopted by many cultures as symbols of fidelity and love. Once they have bonded, they stay together for life. Their body language is very elaborate and they have at least 90 different displays. They dance at all ages, and there are particular dances for courtship and breeding.

"A bird does not sing because it has an answer. It sings because it has a song."

Chinese proverb

HOME BUILDERS

Birds need somewhere to incubate and hatch their eggs. Some build structures, such as the blackbird's cup-shaped grass nest. Ducks lay their eggs in shallow depressions in sand, vegetation or earth. Woodpeckers drill holes in trees and shearwaters dig burrows by the sea. The mallee fowl builds a large mound of leaves, adjusting the temperature by adding or scraping away as necessary.

He threads the branc with grasses to form a circular structure between 1m and 10r above the ground.

The male Cape weaver bird first winds grasses and reeds around a branch.

Rooftop nest

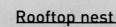

White storks are famous for the large, untidy nests that they build on top of roofs, towers, tall trees, cliff ledges and telephone poles. The birds pair for life and return to the same nest year after year, adding to the nest each time. Some older nests are very large.

> The mallee fowl builds a large nest mound 5m high and 11m wide.

Weaving a home

Weaver birds build the most elaborate nests of any bird. Different species use different materials and create a variety of shapes. For example, sociable weavers build giant, multi-chambered nests, with room for up to 100 families.

The Cape weaver of South Africa uses its long, pointed beak to weave a round nest with a downward-facing entrance.

Burrowing birds

The only time Atlantic puffins spend on land is to nest. They dig out burrows in the soil of grassy cliffs, lining the nest with grass, feathers or seaweed. They produce a single egg and both parents look after the chick until it fledges.

The entrance to the Cape weaver bird's finished nest faces downwards. Inside, the female lays 2 to 5 eggs that she incubates for about two weeks.

Both male and female parents feed the chicks.

Mud structures

Barn swallows build cup-shaped nests from mud pellets that they carry in their beaks from puddles or wet earth in up to 1,000 trips. The nests are often built in barns or under the eaves of a house, and lined with grasses and feathers or other soft materials.

RAISING YOUNG

Birds have evolved strategies to give their young the best chance of survival. There is safety in numbers – crowding together in large colonies works well. Many birds lay large clutches of eggs, or have several batches of young each year. This ensures that even if some chicks die, others survive to adulthood. Within hours of hatching out, many fledglings instinctively follow their parents on food-finding expeditions.

⊖ CUCKOO IN THE NEST

Some cuckoos make another species hatch and look after their chicks. A cuckoo may lay an egg in a warbler's nest that resembles the host's eggs, but the cuckoo hatches earlier and grows faster. Often, the cuckoo chick pushes the eggs or other hatchlings out of the nest, while the parent warblers feed it as if it were their own.

A cuckoo fledgling is fed by its warbler 'parent'.

"In all things of nature there is something of the marvellous."

Aristotle (384–322BCE)
Greek philosopher, from his work On the Parts of Animals *(350BCE)*

Babies on ice

Chicks in the open are in danger of attack from predators. Emperor penguin chicks are also threatened by the icy cold of Antarctica. The parents take it in turns to keep first the egg and then the newly hatched chick safe and warm, tucked in above their feet.

distinctive fluffy orange-and-blue head

unborn coot chick in egg

Father's footsteps

By the time a baby ostrich is a day old, it can eat and walk, and its one aim is to follow the long legs of its parent. If one male with its offspring meets another, they tend to fight. The loser runs away so fast that its young cannot keep up. Instead they follow the victor, who suddenly finds himself with an expanded family!

The aggressive Eurasian coot lives on lakes and rivers throughout Europe, Africa, Asia and Australia.

Nesting on water

Coots build tall nests of dried grasses in reed beds or on underwater obstacles in the middle of lakes and rivers. They lay up to 15 speckled eggs in a clutch, but only a few chicks survive. The rest are taken by predators such as foxes, starve to death or are killed by their own parents when food is scarce.

The parent feeds very young chicks on insect larvae, seeds and plants.

egg tooth used to chip hole in shell

HUNTING SKILLS

PREY - *any animal that is eaten by a predator*

There are no more expert hunters than the birds of prey. They hunt from the air, using their keen senses of sight and hearing to target prey – eagles can spot a moving rabbit at a distance of three kilometres. Peregrines stoop at an incredible 320 kilometres per hour, striking with sharp talons and killing by impact. The nocturnal barn owl is able to find its mouse prey in complete darkness.

The wingspan is up to 1.7m.

Secondary flight feathers give the bird lift.

Powerful scavenger

Like vultures, Marabou storks have naked heads and necks, adaptations for scavenging. These large birds are up to 1.4m high and weigh up to 8kg. They seek out all kinds of prey, both alive and dead, and if their heads were covered in feathers, it would be difficult to keep them clean.

Absolute control

The smaller a hummingbird is, the faster its wings beat. When a 10cm-long buff-bellied hummingbird sips nectar from a flower, its wings beat at an amazing 40 times per second. These birds' wings allow them to fly forwards, up and down, sideways and backwards.

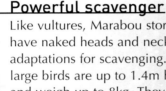

Hummingbirds have such control that they can hover on the spot.

> The Australian pelican has the longest beak at up to 47cm.

barbule

arb

losely linked
arbs and
arbules form
smooth
urface for flight.

Flight feathers are long and
stiff, giving the bird lift and
allowing it to manoeuvre.

Primary feathers
propel the bird
through the air.

The Eurasian
kingfisher has
dazzling blue
and orange
plumage.

A strongly curved
beak tears fish apart.

Snatching prey

The poise and control of the hunting bird
can be seen clearly when the magnificent
osprey catches its favourite fish food. It flies
low over the water's surface, then plunges
feet-first, sometimes right into the water,
its talons outstretched to snatch up a fish.

⊖ BEAK SHAPES

All birds have beaks that
are specially adapted to
find the food that will
enable them to survive in
a particular environment.
For example, some have
hard tips to kill prey or
crack nuts, while others
have sensitive tips to
locate food by touch.

A parrot's strong,
curved beak
breaks into
nuts and fruit to
extract the seeds.

A pelican dives, using
its pouch as a fishing
net. It tips its beak to
drain the water then
eats the fish whole.

The flamingo swings
its upside-down beak
from side to side in
water, filtering out
small food items.

Diving for food

Kingfishers have a dramatic
hunting method. They sit still on
a branch above a stream, waiting
for signs of movement. Then they
dive swiftly and steeply into the
water, capturing the fish in their
dagger-shaped beak at a depth
of no more than 25cm. They beat
their wings to resurface, returning
to their perch to eat their prey.

INVESTIGATE

You can spot birds in your garden or at a local park but wildlife centres, museums and zoos help you to understand more about the species you are watching.

Aviaries and zoos

At an aviary, zoo or wildlife centre, you will be able to see birds from around the world and learn more about these beautiful creatures.

The Summer tanager has a melodic call.

 RSPB Pocket Guide to British Birds by Simon Harrap (A & C Black)

 Flying High Bird Sanctuary, Cnr Bruce Highway & Old Creek Road, Apple Tree Creek, Queensland 4660, Australia

www.allaboutbirds.org

Books and magazines

Take a trip to the library to browse the vast selection of books about birds or find out about specialist bird magazines.

 RSPB British Birds of Prey by Marianne Taylor (Christopher Helm)

 Bookstores in museums, zoos and wildlife centres usually have a great range of books about species that you can see in their exhibits to help you find out more about them.

 www.rspb.org.uk

A kingfisher dives to snatch a fish from a freshwater river.

Museums and exhibitions

Museums often have models or preserved specimens of species that have become extinct and are good places to learn about conservation.

In the mating season, the male Mandarin duck acquires a bright plumage.

 The Life of Birds by David Attenborough (BBC Books)

 Slimbridge Wetland Centre, Gloucestershire GL2 7BT

 www.brightonmuseums.org.uk/booth/

The ostrich has long eye-lashes to protect its eyes from dust and sand.

Documentaries and movies

Take to the skies with incredible documentaries and films that will let you see exactly how birds live, feed and breed in the wild.

 The Life of Birds (BBC Films)

 www.youtube.com is a great place to find short movies featuring birds from all over the world. Check out www.youtube.com/watch?v=Dbo3eoNN5tc

 www.birdlife.org.au

REPTILES AND AMPHIBIANS

REPTILE SENSES

"Use your enemy's hand
to catch a snake."

Persian proverb

Most reptiles are skilled at spotting moving prey. There are some, such as blind snakes, that have only poor eyesight because they live underground. Snakes do not have an ear opening and can only hear very low sounds, feeling sound through their bodies as they slither along. Many reptiles use their tongue to touch, and some snakes use it to taste.

brain

nerve

forked tongue

Jacobson's
organ

The viper's forked tongue rubs off the scents it has collected onto the Jacobson's organ in the roof of the mouth. The organ analyses the scents and sends a message to the brain.

A slender anole lizard is quite unaware of the danger it is in. One lunge by the viper and it is all over.

The deeper the fork in the tongue, the more the Jacobson's organ is used.

> Special ligaments in a snake's jaw allow it to swallow prey many times bigger than the size of its head.

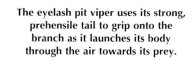

The eyelash pit viper uses its strong, prehensile tail to grip onto the branch as it launches its body through the air towards its prey.

Sensing food

An eyelash pit viper – so-called because of the spiny scales over each eye – strikes, its mouth open to give a venomous bite. The forked tongue, flicking in and out and tasting the air, has detected the scent of potential prey. On the front of its face, heat sensors called pits have indicated the exact location and size of the anole lizard.

Hunting with a lure

There are two red structures on the tip of an alligator snapping turtle's tongue. These wriggle like small worms, acting as a lure for swimming prey. All this North American turtle has to do is sit on the bottom of a river with its mouth open and wait for a fish to swim in.

A THIRD EYE

New Zealand's tuataras are called 'living fossils' because they have hardly changed in 200 million years. They have a tiny third 'eye' on the top of the head. It is visible in hatchlings, but is then covered with scales. The eye is connected to the pineal gland and may, by interpreting the amount of light falling on it, trigger sleep and hibernation.

Scary senses

A snake can sense vibrations through the ground, alerting it to nearby prey. It also picks up scents with its tongue. The tongue wipes airborne particles on to the roof of the mouth, where special cells send messages to the snake's brain that allow it to identify the scent.

Diamondback rattlesnake is named for its diamond-shaped markings.

Tail rattle makes sound to warn off predators.

VENOMOUS SNAKES

With its slithering body and lightning speed, the snake is one of the most feared hunters. Many venomous snakes lie in wait for prey. When a victim comes near, the snake rears up and strikes, injecting lethal venom from its fangs. Venom is a clever means of attack, hijacking dangerous prey with little physical contact. The poison paralyses or kills quickly, and may even begin to break down the body for digestion.

 Australia is home to 11 of the top 12 most venomous land snakes.

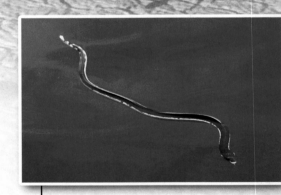

Sea snakes

Found in tropical waters, sea snakes are among the most poisonous reptiles. Luckily, they rarely come into contact with people and are not aggressive. One exception is the beaked sea snake of Australia. It carries out 90 per cent of fatal sea snake attacks.

Spraying venom

As well as injecting prey, a cobra spits venom to defend itself. It can hit an enemy's eyes from as far away as 2.4m, causing temporary blindness.

● CAMOUFLAGED KILLERS

With no limbs, many snakes cannot chase prey. Instead, they wait for prey to come to them. They have such excellent camouflage that they are almost impossible to see, especially as they keep so still. Depending on their habitat, snakes have colours and markings that blend in with leaves, vines, sand or rock.

A gaboon viper's markings resemble leaf litter.

Snake detects smells with its nostrils, as well as with the cells of the Jacobson's organ in the mouth.

Venom

Special glands produce the venom, which is squeezed along tiny tubes into the hollow fangs. The venom is forced through tiny openings in the fangs and injected into puncture wounds made by the sharp fang tips.

collared lizard

Forked tongue collects scent particles from the air as it flicks to and fro.

"When you see a rattlesnake poised to strike you, do not wait until he has struck before you crush him."

Franklin D. Roosevelt (1882–1945)
US President, 1933–1945

CONSTRICTOR CREW

Constrictors, such as boas, pythons and anacondas, kill with power not poison. When these snakes strike, they rapidly throw muscular coils around their prey's body. Each time the victim breathes out, the coils tighten a little more, so that it cannot breathe in. The tight squeeze also stops the prey's blood flowing. Unable to pump blood, the heart comes to a fatal standstill.

A mouse's fate

While suffocating its prey, a boa constrictor keeps a firm grip with sharp, hooked teeth. These teeth are no use for chewing, though, so the boa must swallow its victim whole.

⊖ EXPLODING PYTHON

In 2005, in Everglades National Park in Florida, USA, the remains of an alligator were found sticking out of a dead Burmese python. The snake's stomach had been ripped open by the alligator's claws.

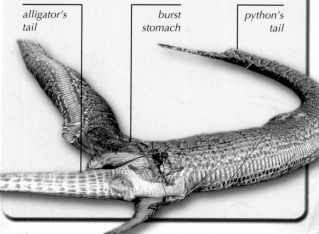

alligator's tail   burst stomach   python's tail

South American giant

The anaconda is the world's heaviest snake, weighing 200kg or more. It lives in or near water, catching capybaras and other animals that come to drink, as well as river turtles and caimans.

A young red-tail boa constricts a mouse.

backwards-facing teeth to drag in food

breathing tube

jaws joined by stretchy ligaments

Stretchy jaws

A snake's jaws are joined by ligaments that stretch to give it the necessary gape to eat its super-sized meals. The snake can breathe with its mouth full because it has a movable breathing tube at the front of the lower jaw.

Constrictor's ribs can move apart to make room for swallowed prey.

"None of them knew the limits of [Kaa the python's] power, none of them could look him in the face, and none had ever come alive out of his hug."

Rudyard Kipling (1865–1936)
From the novel **The Jungle Book** *(1894)*

Down in one

A boa usually swallows prey headfirst, so the legs do not get stuck in its throat. The snake coats its dinner with slippery saliva, then uses strong muscles to push the food into its stomach. Here, powerful juices dissolve the flesh and bones.

http://animals.nationalgeographic.com/animals/reptiles/boa-constrictor.html

DANGEROUS AMPHIBIANS

The world's most poisonous animal is a small amphibian from the rainforests of Colombia. To deter predators, the golden poison-dart frog has deadly toxins in its skin that attack the nervous system, rapidly causing heart failure. The cane toad is another amphibian that produces poisons in its skin for self defence.

Poisonous toad

The cane toad, a native of Central and South America, is seriously poisonous. Glands on its shoulders produce a milky poison, containing a deadly cocktail of 14 chemicals that cause convulsions and death. Introduced into Australia in the 1930s to control insect pests, the 2kg toad is now poisoning rare native species.

reservoir of milky poison

Poison glands lie under the warty skin.

Rodent is devoured headfirst by the hungry toad, whose diet also includes insects and small reptiles.

> Poison-dart frogs get their name because the Chocó people of Central America rub the poison onto the darts they use for hunting.

An ant's body contains poisons – if a frog preys on the ant, the poisons transfer to the frog.

Deadly diet

A poison-dart frog's poison comes from its diet of ants, termites, beetles and centipedes. These minibeasts absorb poisonous chemicals from the plants they eat. Frogs that are moved to a zoo lose their toxicity because they are not eating their natural diet.

Cane toads hunt at night. They locate prey by noticing movement or by tracking their scent.

Colour code

In daylight hours this poison-dart frog is protected by its colours and pattern, which warn other animals that it is best left alone. After dark, predators such as this tarantula are warned off by the taste of the frog's skin.

green poison-dart frog and tarantula

golden poison-dart frog

http://nationalzoo.si.edu/Animals/Amazonia/Facts/fact-poisondartfrog.cfm

● HOW TOXIC ARE THEY?

A golden poison-dart frog is just 5cm long, but its body contains enough poison to kill 10 humans – or an astonishing 25,000 mice. How does that compare with other poisonous creatures?

"Even crocodiles have been found dead with cane toads in their mouths."

Mary Summerill (born 1958)
Presenter of the BBC documentary series
Wild Down Under *(2003)*

Golden poison-dart frog could kill 25,000 mice.

Black widow spider could kill 700 mice.

King cobra could kill 3,500 mice.

Glides over distances of up to 60m have been recorded.

Flying from danger

When this tree-dwelling flying lizard is threatened, it has an unusual method of escape. It has elongated ribs with skin stretched between them, which act like wings as it glides from tree to tree. When the lizard is at rest, the ribs fold against the body.

⊖ WARNING COLORATION

When strong contrasting colours are seen on an animal, they usually warn that the animal is dangerous. Most of the non-venomous milksnakes have bright red, black and yellow bands. These colours mimic those of the highly venomous coral snake, and the milksnake sometimes even copies the coral snake's behaviour to scare away predators.

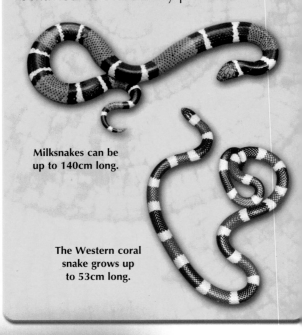

Milksnakes can be up to 140cm long.

The Western coral snake grows up to 53cm long.

AVOIDING PREDATORS

Reptiles have very varied ways of protecting themselves. Like other animals, they often run away, climb trees or fight back when attacked. However, many are superbly camouflaged and even able to change colour. Some lizards can shed part of their tail if seized, growing a new one in its place. Reptiles such as the frilled lizard can make themselves look bigger, and the hard shells of turtles and tortoises are an effective defence.

A thorny problem

The thorny devil's colour changes from pale browns when warm to darker colours when cold, and this camouflage is very effective in the deserts of Australia. However, it is slow-moving and would be vulnerable to predators if it were not covered all over with sharp spines.

The thorny devil rocks backwards and forwards as it walks.

 > Texas horned lizards squirt blood from ducts near their eyes at predators up to 3m away.

The distinctive curled muscular tail has adapted to grasp and balance.

Masters of disguise

Panther chameleons can be found all over the island of Madagascar, off the southeast coast of Africa. They vary in colour, and the males are generally more brightly coloured than the females. Like all chameleons, they change colour in response to changes in temperature, light or mood.

brightly coloured adult male panther chameleon

www.boredpanda.com/animal-camouflage

Chameleons are difficult to spot in leafy rainforest habitat.

"A chameleon doesn't leave one tree until he's sure of another."

Arabian proverb

Faking death

One defensive mechanism used by some animals when threatened is to play dead. A reptile that does this very effectively is the shy and elusive grass snake. It becomes completely limp, turning on its back with its mouth open and tongue lolling out.

SELF-PROTECTION

TOXIN – *a poison made by living cells or organisms that can cause disease*

It is a dangerous world, and animals need to defend themselves. Some attack before they can be attacked. Many are armed with horns, sharp teeth, quills, claws or great strength. Some give off powerful smells or simply run away quickly, while others adopt frightening poses. Many amphibians are brightly coloured or have poisonous skin that tastes nasty to a predator. There are even toads that play dead!

"Swallow a toad in the morning and you will encounter nothing more disgusting the rest of the day."

Nicolas de Chamfort (1741–94)
French writer and wit

Marine toads can be up to 25cm in length and over 2kg in weight.

Poisonous prey

The world's largest toad lives in the open grasslands and woodlands of Central and South America and Australia. Called the marine toad and cane toad, it is prey to snakes, caimans, birds of prey and black rats. If squeezed in their jaws, the toad oozes highly toxic fluid. However, many of its predators are immune to this poison.

Fire salamanders are nocturnal, searching for their insect prey on the forest floor at night.

Poisonous defence

The fire salamander has large glands behind its eyes and down the back on either side of the spine. If the animal is threatened, the glands produce a milky defensive chemical called salamandrin. This poison is strong enough to kill small animals.

> The 5cm-long golden poison dart frog has enough venom to kill ten grown men.

Bufotoxins from glands on shoulders contain 14 chemicals.

⊖ PLAYING DEAD

When threatened, the Surinam toad (above) and the leopard frog may play dead by keeping still. The Surinam toad is particularly convincing because it is almost completely flat in shape and looks like a leaf. It also uses this ability to hunt, lying still on the bottom of streams to ambush prey.

http://animals.nationalgeographic.com/animals/amphibians/golden-poison-dart-frog.html

Poisonous frogs

The poison arrow frogs of Central and South America are protected effectively against predators such as snakes and spiders. The frogs are brilliantly coloured, and these 'warning colours' alert predators to the dangers of trying to pick them up and eat them. The frogs also secrete deadly toxins from their skin.

strawberry poison arrow frog in the rainforest

The Komodo uses its tongue to sniff out potential meals

Saliva contains more than 60 types of bacteria.

A Komodo can weigh up to 200kg – more than two grown men.

Deadly saliva

Komodo dragons produce saliva full of harmful bacteria, which works as a primitive venom. If prey is wounded but manages to escape, it will die from the infected wound, and the dragon will find and eat it.

LETHAL LIZARDS

Most lizards are carnivorous, but two species have serious bites that can be dangerous to humans. One is the Gila (pronounced 'heela') monster, which lives in deserts in Mexico and southwestern USA. The other is a huge monitor lizard, the Komodo dragon, whose mouth is full of deadly bacteria. The world's largest lizard, it lives on four islands in Indonesia.

⊖ FATAL ATTACK

Tragically, in 2007 a Komodo killed an eight-year-old boy. The animal mauled and bit the child, shaking him viciously from side to side. His family drove off the dragon but the boy died from massive bleeding.

thick, strong neck

scaly, leathery hide

powerful limbs

> The Komodo dragon can detect a potential meal from 5km away, using its flicking tongue to sniff the air.

Scary monster

The Gila monster is a slow-moving lizard. It tries to avoid confrontation if it can by hissing at any animals that challenge it. As a last resort, the Gila will bite, chewing to activate glands in its jaw to produce a poisonous saliva. The toxins, which flow in through the wound, cause paralysis. The Gila's eye-catching colour and skin patterns warn enemies that it is poisonous.

Dinner for six

Six Komodo dragons devour a goat. Komodos move swiftly for their size, and attack water buffaloes, boars and deer. They pin down and rip apart prey with their massive claws. Unfussy diners, Komodos eat carrion too.

www.amnh.org/exhibitions/past-exhibitions/lizards-and-snakes-alive

Bead-like, scaly skin is black with pink and yellow markings.

Baby rats are attacked by a Gila monster.

"The breath is very fetid and its odour can be detected at some little distance."

Scientific American **magazine, 1890**

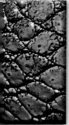

CROCODILIAN – a member of a group of reptiles that includes crocodiles, alligators and gharials

KILLER CROCODILIANS

They look like prehistoric beasts, but crocodiles and alligators are very much alive, lurking in rivers and lakes. These reptiles are found in subtropical and tropical parts of the world, where the sun warms their cold-blooded bodies and turns them into agile hunters. The saltwater crocodile can grow as long as five metres. It devours fish, other crocodiles, birds, mammals – and unlucky humans.

Big snapper
The gharial nimbly catches fish by sweeping the water with its long, narrow snout. Its needle-like teeth are perfect for spearing slippery prey.

Deadly grip
A Nile crocodile clamps its jaws around a gazelle's neck in a Kenyan game park. Prey this large is a challenge for crocodiles because they cannot chew. They have to spin a kill until it breaks apart.

> Crocodiles and alligators are believed to kill about 2,000 people every year.

Nostril is set high on the skull, so that the crocodile can breathe when hiding in water.

Leathery skin is reinforced with bony, armoured plates called scutes.

New teeth for old

Crocodiles have around 60 teeth. They are designed for grabbing prey rather than cutting flesh. So, to help break down large chunks of meat, crocodilians swallow stones. These churn around in one part of their stomach, grinding up the food.

> **"Don't think there are no crocodiles because the water is calm."**
>
> **Malayan proverb**

● SHOCK ATTACK

A crocodile's eyes, ears and nostrils are on the top of its head, allowing it to lie low in the water and still see, hear, smell and breathe. To save energy crocodiles wait, motionless, until a meal approaches...

Resembling a log in the river, this Nile crocodile is unseen by its prey – a zebra on its way down to drink.

The crocodile explodes out of the water in a lethal burst, clamping its jaws around the zebra's muzzle.

The terrified zebra slips on the muddy riverbank. Unable to struggle free, it is dragged into deeper water.

The crocodile spins the victim, drowning it or smashing its spine, then breaking the body into chunks.

www.crocodilian.com

The 60cm-long Gila monster lives in North America and has a large tail to store fat, which it can live off for months at a time.

Legs are set in the sides of the body.

Alternate legs move together.

Lizard 'tastes' air with its tongue.

Short, sturdy legs and long claws are good for digging.

UNDER THE SKIN

Locomotion in reptiles depends on what is happening under the skin. Snakes have no legs, so they use their ribs and muscles to slither along the ground or move from branch to branch. Some snakes 'sidewind' on sand, throwing themselves across the loose surface diagonally. Reptiles such as lizards are more slow and restricted, using their strong limbs and tails to move. The slowest of all on land are the armoured turtles and tortoises.

Walk like a lizard

Lizards, including this Gila monster, move more like a fish than a mammal. They sway as they walk, and the muscles that move their bodies from side to side are the same ones that help them to breathe. They are not able to run as efficiently as mammals. Lizards are good at running in short bursts, but only if their bodies are warm. If they are cold, they move much more slowly.

> Some basilisk lizards can run away on their hind legs across the water's surface when threatened.

http://kids.yahoo.com/animals/reptiles

⊖ VERTICAL RUN

Geckos are impressive climbers. They are able to run vertically up most surfaces and even upside down across overhanging areas. They have flattened pads at the ends of their toes that are covered with millions of microscopic hairs called setae, each split into branches. These help to 'glue' the lizards to nearly any surface.

Tokay geckos are often seen running up and down the walls of houses in southeast Asia, chasing the insects and small invertebrates that they eat.

Unlike most lizards, the tail does not grow back when broken.

Gila monsters live in scrubland and desert, burrowing into thickets and under rocks to find moisture and escape the heat.

The spine is long and flexible.

Gila monster can give a venomous bite.

Changing skin

Both snakes and lizards moult or 'slough' regularly to replace old or damaged outer skin. Most lizards lose their skin in flakes over a period of days. Snakes, such as this common tiger snake, crawl out of their old skin in one go, turning it inside out and leaving it in one piece.

Venom is produced in salivary glands in the lizard's lower jaw and its poisonous bite is used to defend itself.

INVESTIGATE

Get hands on with reptiles and amphibians and explore more of their natural worlds by checking out wildlife parks, books, websites and museums.

Wildlife parks and zoos

Visit a wildlife park or zoo and see some of the extraordinary variety of reptiles and amphibians that live on Earth. Get close to a poisonous dart frog, a snake or a crocodile.

 100 Facts: Reptiles and Amphibians by Ann Kay (Miles Kelly)

 Amazon World Zoo Park, Isle of Wight PO36 0LX

 www.australiazoo.com.au

This baby American alligator will eventually grow to be as long as a car.

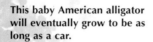

The banded sea krait is a venomous sea snake found in tropical Southeast Asian waters.

Books and magazines

Discover all kinds of facts about amphibians and reptiles for yourself by reading magazines and information books.

 Discover Science: Reptiles by Belinda Weber (Kingfisher)

 Visit your local library to discover a whole range of books about reptiles and amphibians.

 http://kids.sandiegozoo.org/animals/amphibians

The cane toad secrete nasty toxin to de predato

Museums and exhibitions

Natural history museums have displays and expert information about different species, as well as stuffed specimens. Look out for themed exhibitions too.

A fully grown alligator looks for a spot to bask in the Florida everglades.

 Deadly Factbook 3: Reptiles and Amphibians by Steve Backshall (Orion)

 Natural History Museum, Cromwell Road, London SW7 5BD

 www.museum.manchester.ac.uk/kids/galleries/liveanimals

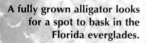

Documentaries and movies

Award-winning documentaries and films allow you to watch reptiles and amphibians displaying natural behaviour in their own habitats.

 Check out the National Geographic reptiles collection at http://video.nationalgeographic.com/video/animals/reptiles

 IMAX 3D cinema, Science Museum, Exhibition Road, South Kensington, London SW7 2DD

 www.bbc.co.uk/nature/life/Reptile

FISH

SWIMMING AND BUOYANCY

BUOYANCY - the power to stay afloat in liquid

Fish swim smoothly through water by contracting and relaxing muscles on each side of their body. This causes waves of movement to travel from the head towards the tail, propelling the fish forwards. Different shaped tails help fish travel at different rates. Pectoral and pelvic fins help fish move, manoeuvre and stop. Some fish even use them to swim backwards. To control buoyancy, most fish are equipped with a gas-filled organ called the swim bladder.

> "This is the Ocean, silly, we're not the only two in here."
>
> **Dory**
> *Fictional fish in the film* Finding Nemo *(2003)*

Pectoral fins flap like wings.

Wings under water

Manta rays have larger pectoral fins than most fish and they travel by gracefully flapping them like wings. They feed on plankton and fish larvae filtered from the water passing through their gills. Instead of a swim bladder, rays and sharks have an oil-filled liver that prevents them from sinking.

> Male seahorses carry their young in pouches until they are ready to give birth.

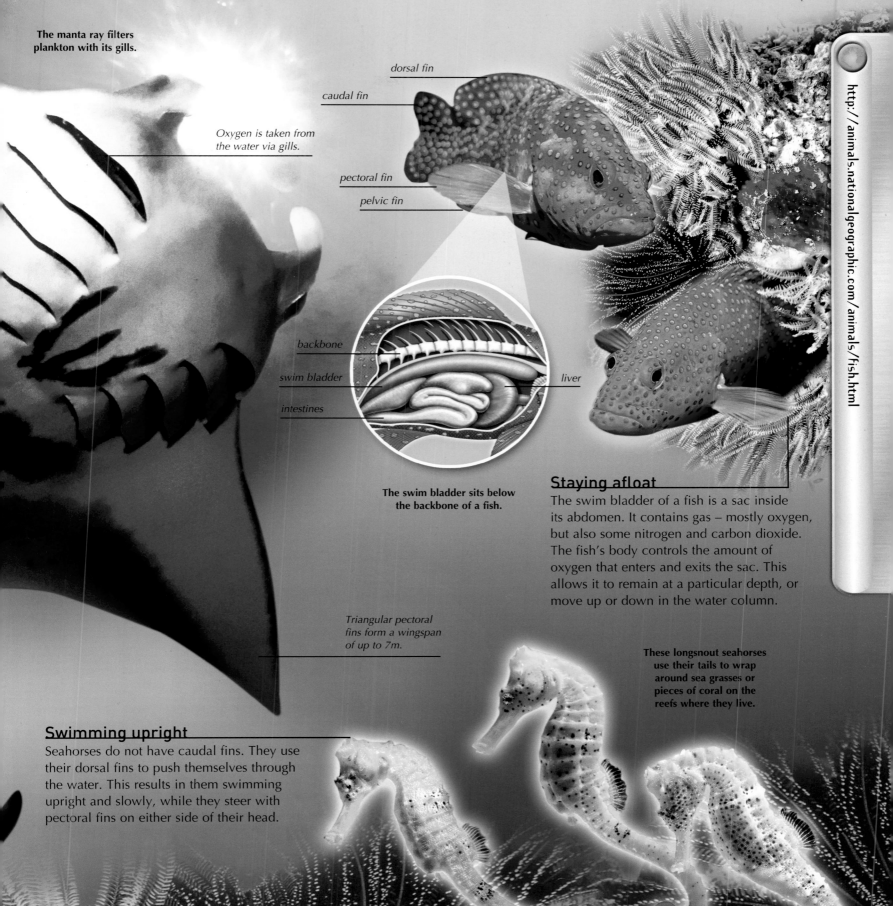

The manta ray filters plankton with its gills.

dorsal fin

caudal fin

Oxygen is taken from the water via gills.

pectoral fin

pelvic fin

backbone

swim bladder

intestines

liver

The swim bladder sits below the backbone of a fish.

Staying afloat

The swim bladder of a fish is a sac inside its abdomen. It contains gas – mostly oxygen, but also some nitrogen and carbon dioxide. The fish's body controls the amount of oxygen that enters and exits the sac. This allows it to remain at a particular depth, or move up or down in the water column.

Triangular pectoral fins form a wingspan of up to 7m.

These longsnout seahorses use their tails to wrap around sea grasses or pieces of coral on the reefs where they live.

Swimming upright

Seahorses do not have caudal fins. They use their dorsal fins to push themselves through the water. This results in them swimming upright and slowly, while they steer with pectoral fins on either side of their head.

ATOLL – a coral island shaped like a ring, with a lagoon in the middle of it

CORAL REEFS

"Every one must be struck with astonishment, when he first beholds one of these vast rings of coral-rock, often many leagues in diameter..."

Charles Darwin (1809–82)
The Structure and Distribution of Coral Reefs (1842)

Coral reefs flourish in shallow, clean waters in the tropics. These solid structures are built up from the remains of marine animals called corals. Reefs grow slowly as the animals that form their living surfaces multiply, spread and die, adding their skeletons to the reef. Many people rely on reefs as a source of food and tourist income. The reefs also protect coasts from wave erosion. Some islands are made entirely of coral.

Prickly predator

A hungry crown-of-thorns starfish climbs up on coral and pulls its stomach out of its mouth and over its prey. The starfish releases digestive juices that dissolve the coral down to its skeleton, then the starfish's stomach absorbs nutrients from the liquefied bits.

Underwater garden

A healthy reef bursts with life and colour in much the same way as a rainforest does on land. Even the smallest reefs are teeming with hundreds of different types of corals, fish, crabs, starfish, sea urchins and other animals. Sadly, reefs are under threat from human activity. They are broken up for building materials, damaged by divers and suffer the poisonous effects of coastal pollution.

> Some coral reefs have been growing for about 50 million years, and are over 1km thick.

FORMATION OF A CORAL ATOLL

Coral reefs often fringe volcanic islands where the water is warm, shallow and light. As the islands are worn away by geological processes and sink, more coral grows on top of existing coral to stay in the warmer, lighter surface waters and a barrier reef builds up. A lagoon, or wide stretch of water, separates the coral reef from the island. The island continues to sink. When it disappears completely, a coral atoll is left behind.

coral encircles island

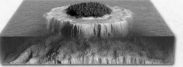

island is reduced

coral ring remains

Danger in the dark

When night falls, whitetip reef sharks emerge from sandy coral caves and burst into frenzied activity, seeking out coral fish hidden deep in the reef. These nocturnal creatures are among the largest predators on reefs.

KEY

1 Queen angelfish

2 Clownfish

3 Giant sea anemone

4 Crown-of-thorns starfish

5 Yellow cube boxfish

6 Lionfish

7 Queen angelfish

IN THE DEEP

Light does not penetrate beyond a few hundred metres below the surface of Earth's oceans. In these dark and hostile waters live some of the strangest creatures on the planet. Many of them are fierce predators, with sharp teeth, flexible jaws and unusual hunting strategies. Living at great depths, they are seldom seen and little is known about their life cycles.

When the tiny 6mm-long male bearded anglerfish finds a female, he bites into her skin and fuses with her, becoming part of her body. This means that, when she is ready to spawn, there is a mate immediately available.

> **PHOTOPHORE** - *a light-producing organ found in some deep-sea fish*

Anglerfish can move and light up their lures when needed.

A 10cm-long female bearded anglerfish, or illuminated netdevil, floats motionless. The bioluminescent lure on its head and barbel (beard) hanging from its chin attract prey towards its gaping jaws.

Elaborate barbel resembles a piece of seaweed, attracting shrimps and other prey.

Light in the darkness

Deep-sea fish have adapted in many varied ways to the different depths at which they live. Some species have special organs called photophores that give off bioluminescent light – a light produced by a chemical reaction. Other species have 'fishing-rods' that act as lures, or long feelers that help them seek out prey.

Circular photophores behind each eye illuminate the water with a red glow.

The stoplight loosejaw dragonfish is unusual – it can produce and see red light. In depths of up to 2,500m, it also produces green light from a comma-shaped

The living fossil

In 1938, an unusual fish was caught in the western Indian Ocean. It was identified as a coelacanth, which was thought to have been extinct for at least 65 million years. Coelacanths can be up to 2m long and live at depths of up to 700m.

A third 'leg' is formed from extended tail fin.

The tripodfish lives at the bottom of the ocean. To catch prey, it 'stands' on the sea floor, facing into the current and waiting for small crustaceans to be swept towards it.

Front 'legs' are formed from extended pelvic fins.

The underside is covered in glowing photophores.

The cookiecutter shark has been found in water up to 3,500m below the surface. This small shark attaches itself to prey such as a whale and spins to cut out a cookie-shaped plug of flesh.

Deep-sea shark

This rarely seen frilled shark looks more like an eel than a shark. It has 300 distinctive pronged teeth and an extraordinary curved tail fin. It is up to 2m long and hunts fish, squid and other sharks at depths of up to 1,500m. This species has changed very little since prehistoric times.

❯ The black seadevil anglerfish is the size of a tennis ball.

PREDATORY PIRANHAS

Piranhas are small freshwater fish that live in the rivers of South America. They have strong, upturned jaws like those of a bulldog, and remarkably sharp teeth. Not all species of piranha are aggressive, but those that are have a fearsome reputation. When they are hungry and gang up in a school, they work together as one ferocious killing machine, targeting birds, rodents, frogs and young caimans.

Caught by a caiman
A shoal of 20–30 piranhas may be a threat to a young caiman, but this lone fish stands no chance against a fully grown black caiman.

An excited piranha turns on another. Even though these fish hunt together, within the shoal it is every fish for itself.

In the dry season, piranhas can be stranded in small lakes with little food. This makes them more aggressive.

⊖ KILLER JAWS

A piranha's upper and lower teeth fit together so neatly that they can remove a perfect, crescent-shaped chunk of flesh. Amazonian Indians have used the razor-sharp teeth for sharpening darts, shaving and cutting.

The jaw is packed with triangular teeth.

> In Brazil about 1,200 cattle are killed by piranhas every year.

Feeding frenzy

A young heron has fallen from its treetop nest into the river. Within seconds, its struggles have alerted a shoal of red-bellied piranhas. Smaller fish size up the prey, taking a few test bites before larger piranhas drag the bird below the surface.

www.extremescience.com/piranha.htm

Nostrils can detect a single drop of blood in 200 litres of water.

INVESTIGATE

Discover all about the inhabitants of the ocean by visiting aquariums, museums and wildlife parks or finding out more in books or on the Internet.

Aquariums and zoos

There are lots of opportunities to come face to face with a shark or a piranha in an aquarium or zoo. Some even offer swimming with sharks experiences!

A whale shark entertains visitors to the Okinawa Aquarium, Japan.

 Weird Sea Creatures by Laura Marsh (National Geographic Society)

 National Aquarium of New Zealand, Marine Parade, Napier, New Zealand

 www.sharktrust.co.uk/en/shark_factsheets

Books and magazines

Libraries are great places to find out all sorts of strange and interesting facts about deep sea creatures.

 Dangerous Animals of the Sea by Samantha Flores (Amazon)

 Museum and aquarium book shops have specialist books with amazing photos and lots of interesting information.

 ocean.nationalgeographic.com/ocean/photos/dangerous-sea-creatures

A crown-of-thorns seastar feeds on coral in the Andaman Sea.

Museums and exhibitions

Many museums have amazing exhibits where you can see just how big sea creatures are in real life by standing next to them.

 Creatures of the Deep by John Woodward (Natural History Museum)

 Shark Walk and Shark Valley, Sea Life Sydney Aquarium, 1–5 Wheat Road, Sydney, New South Wales, Australia

 www.bristolzoo.org.uk/fish

The queen angelfish lives among reefs in the Caribbean Sea.

The green sea turtle migrates thousands of kilometres each year.

Documentaries and movies

Dive into the oceans with the amazing documentaries and films which will take you right into these creatures' worlds – without even getting wet.

 Blue Planet (BBC Films)

 www.youtube.com is a great place to find short movies about dangerous underwater creatures. Check out https://www.youtube.com/watch?v=PQfSF6hKYIU

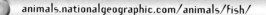 animals.nationalgeographic.com/animals/fish/

INVERTEBRATES

LONG-DISTANCE TRAVEL

MIGRATION - the long-distance movement of an animal from one place to another

⊜ A PLAGUE OF LOCUSTS

The migratory locust migrates when its food supply becomes irregular, usually due to the weather. Swarms are sometimes carried by the wind for up to 500km in a single night, and when they land, they eat all the vegetation over a vast area. They travel in huge swarms – the largest known contained about 40 billion insects.

Some invertebrates travel great distances at particular times of the year. These migrations can range from a few kilometres to several thousand kilometres. Changes in weather and temperature play an important role in stimulating many animals to travel. Some migrations are two-way journeys, with the migrants or their offspring returning to particular breeding areas every year. Some journeys are not controlled by the invertebrates, but by the tides or winds.

Spiny lobsters set out on their annual migration in the Bahamas.

They follow the light-coloured spots on the lobster in front of them.

"Not all those who wander are lost."

J. R. R. Tolkien (1892–1973)
British writer, from his novel,
The Fellowship of the Ring (1954)

> In 1988 desert locusts were blown 4,500km from Africa to the West Indies by unusually powerful winds.

One by one

Once a year, large numbers of spiny lobsters move in single file across the sea floor on a migration that takes them from shallow to deep water. In spring, the spawning season, adult females lay thousands of eggs in warm, coastal areas. Their extraordinary journey usually takes place in the autumn, when the lobsters travel to deep water for the winter.

They keep contact with one another by using their antennae.

Tiny travellers

Vertical migration happens in oceans and rivers. Some of the smallest creatures, zooplankton, travel up and down in the water, their movements triggered by light levels. At dusk, they reach the surface to graze on phytoplankton overnight.

Clouds of butterflies

Every year, clouds of beautiful monarch butterflies travel 3,200km from southern Canada to the warmth of central Mexico, where they spend the winter. The following spring, they or their offspring return to Canada, laying eggs on the way.

http://spaceplace.nasa.gov/migration/redirected/

AMBUSH!

Predatory invertebrates lie in wait for prey, often using camouflage to great effect. Some brightly coloured crab spiders look exactly like a flower, and inject a powerful poison to kill insects larger than themselves. Assassin bugs stab flies, mosquitoes and caterpillars, paralysing them. And ichneumon wasps parasitise their prey, laying their eggs in the larvae and pupae of other insects. The larvae eat their hosts from the inside.

⊖ STABBED TO DEATH

Robber flies sit very still somewhere where they can see all around them with their large eyes. When potential food flies past, these large flies (up to 5cm in length) spring off their perch and capture their prey in flight. They have a strong, piercing proboscis and spiny legs that help them hold onto struggling prey.

A robber fly sucks at its blue beetle prey.

an orchid mantis on
an orchid flower
in Malaysia

*The mantis lies
in wait looking
exactly like a petal.*

*An unsuspecting
fly is seized
when it lands.*

Predatory mantis

One of the most extraordinary animal camouflages is that of the praying mantis – so-called because it holds its front legs up as if it is 'praying'. These insects live in tropical areas and individual species are often camouflaged to match plants in their habitat.

> There are about 37,500 different known species of spiders in the world.

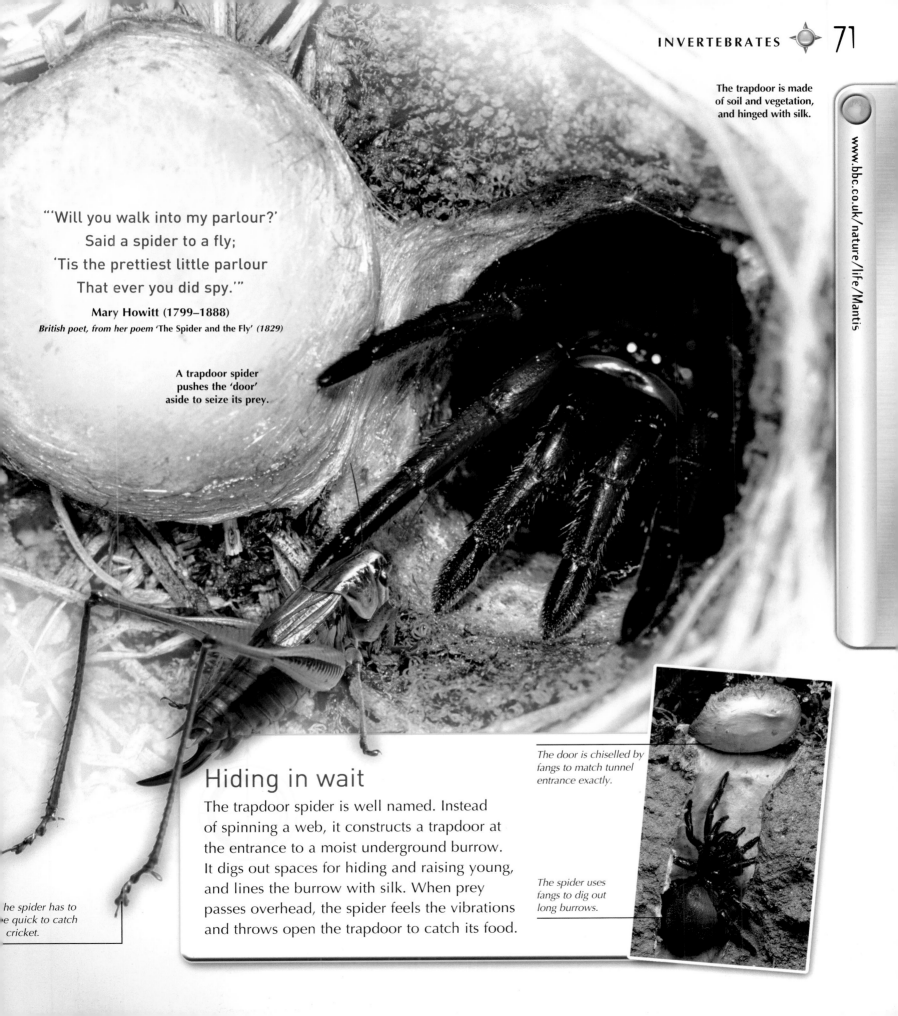

The trapdoor is made of soil and vegetation, and hinged with silk.

www.bbc.co.uk/nature/life/Mantis

"'Will you walk into my parlour?'
Said a spider to a fly;
'Tis the prettiest little parlour
That ever you did spy.'"

Mary Howitt (1799–1888)
British poet, from her poem 'The Spider and the Fly' *(1829)*

A trapdoor spider pushes the 'door' aside to seize its prey.

he spider has to
e quick to catch
cricket.

Hiding in wait

The trapdoor spider is well named. Instead of spinning a web, it constructs a trapdoor at the entrance to a moist underground burrow. It digs out spaces for hiding and raising young, and lines the burrow with silk. When prey passes overhead, the spider feels the vibrations and throws open the trapdoor to catch its food.

The door is chiselled by fangs to match tunnel entrance exactly.

The spider uses fangs to dig out long burrows.

KILLER COLONY

Which animals form an army and eat every creature in their path? Army ants, which live in the Americas. They march on a million feet across the jungle floor. Cockroaches, scorpions, tarantulas, crickets – all run for their lives. When an army ant finds its prey, it releases a chemical that 'calls out' to its comrades. In seconds, hundreds of ants arrive to sting the victim, dismember its body and carry it back to the nest.

ANT IN CLOSE-UP

An ant's body has three parts – a head, thorax and abdomen. The head has the mouth, eyes and antennae. The mouth has two scissor-like jaws called mandibles. Army ants are blind and rely on their antennae to smell, touch and communicate.

thorax

head

abdomen

"Go to the ant, you lazybones; consider its ways, and be wise."

Proverbs 6.6, in the Old Testament of the Bible

Ant food

Army ants feed mainly on other insects, but will kill lizards and snakes. Driver ants, which also form colonies but live in Africa, can smother and kill animals as large as chickens, pigs and goats if they are cooped up or tethered.

www.dandelion.org.uk/dc/ant

Antbirds perch above the ants, ready to pick off insects fleeing the colony.

In a tangle

Ants use their own bodies to build bridges – for example, linking a bivouac to the ground. The individual ants cling together with their clawed feet.

Living nests

As army ants move around the forest, they use their own bodies to build temporary night-time nests called bivouacs. The queen and her eggs are safe in the middle of the mass of ants.

Large robber fly is ready to snatch any injured insects.

Each ant finds its way by detecting chemicals given off by other ants.

Army on the march

A column of army ants snakes across the leaf litter. At the front of the column, the soldiers fan out, covering an area 10m wide. Prey creatures are stung, then hacked to pieces by the ants' jaws. The army makes thousands of kills a day.

STING OF THE SCORPION

Scorpions have stung and killed their prey for more than 400 million years – since long before the age of the dinosaurs. These ruthless and efficient hunters often eat their own weight in insects every day, grasping victims with their pincers then using their sting to inject venom. Some scorpions also spray their venom in self-defence – it is hideously painful if it enters the eye.

Small but deadly

This deathstalker scorpion's venom is dangerous to people, causing pain, fever, breathing difficulties and even death. When it feels threatened, the 10cm-long deathstalker raises its tail and readies its claws to attack.

Protective poison

A scorpion mother looks after her young. She carries her brood on her back for the first few days of their lives, with her poison-tipped tail curled over them to keep enemies at bay.

scorpion eating a blowfly

⊖ HAIRY HUNTER

The rock scorpion lives in southern Africa. It hides in cracks between the rocks by day, coming out to hunt at dusk. Its fine body hairs can detect vibrations made by any nearby spiders and insects.

"Lord! how we suddenly jump,
as Scorpio, or the Scorpion,
stings us in the rear."

Stubb
Second mate on the Pequod in Herman Melville's Moby Dick (1851)

Sting in the tail

A northern scorpion feeds on a blowfly.
Scorpions range in colour from yellow and tan
to brown and black. Like spiders, they belong
to the arachnid family, but they store venom
not in the fangs but in their muscular tail.
The poison glands and sting are in
the tail's last segment.

Muscles swing the sting into
position and rock it to and fro.

Venom is squeezed
out of the sting.

Venom is produced
in tiny venom sacs.

www.bbc.co.uk/nature/life/scorpion

INVESTIGATE

Find out more about creepy crawlies and the environments in which they live by visiting zoos and wildlife parks or by watching and reading about these amazing creatures in documentaries, films and reference books.

Wildlife parks and zoos

Visit your nearest zoo where you can get close to many insects and spiders. If you have a fear of spiders, many places offer the chance to handle less dangerous species to help you overcome it.

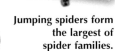
Jumping spiders form the largest of spider families.

 Ultimate Bugopedia by Darlyne Murawski and Nancy Honovich (National Geographic Kids)

 ZSL London Zoo, Regent's Park, London NW1 4RY

 www.scorpionworlds.com

Scorpions use a sting on their tail to paralyse their prey.

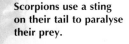

Books and magazines

If you want to know more about creepy crawlies, check out some of the many reference books and magazines at your local library. Your local librarian may also be able to suggest some great books.

 The Big Bug Search by Ian Jackson and Caroline Young (Usborne)

 Ask questions online on the Natural History Museum Bug forum. www.nhm.ac.uk/natureplus/community/identification/bug-forum?fromGateway=true

 http://insects.about.com/od/roachesandmantids/a/10-Fascinating-Facts-About-Praying-Mantids.htm

Museums and exhibitions

Natural history museums have displays and expert information about all sorts of insects and spiders as well as curators to give tours and bring the exhibits to life.

Red wood ants greet each other with jaws touching.

 Spiders: The Ultimate Predators by Stephen Dalton (A & C Black)

 Creepy Crawlies Gallery at the Natural History Museum, Cromwell Road, London SW7 5BD

 www.uksafari.com/spiders.htm

The female praying mantis sometimes eats the male after mating.

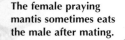

Documentaries and movies

If you can't actually travel to Africa or Australia, do the next best thing and watch documentaries on these places or view photographs by wildlife photographers.

 Madagascar (BBC Films)

 The BBC Nature website has loads of interesting information about invertebrates available for free – www.bbc.co.uk/nature/life/Arachnid

  http://animals.nationalgeographic.com/animals/bugs/seamonsters/

GLOSSARY

abdomen
In animals such as insects and arachnids, the tail end of the body.

algae (sing. alga)
Simple non-flowering plants that grow in water or moist surroundings.

amphibian
A cold-blooded animal that lives on land but breeds in water, for example a frog.

antenna (plural: antennae)
In insects, one of a pair of sensory feelers that stick out from the head.

arachnid
An animal of the class Arachnida, such as a spider or a scorpion. All arachnids have eight legs.

bacterium (plural: bacteria)
A simple micro-organism. Some bacteria can cause disease.

bioluminescence
The production of light by living things, found in fish and insects as well as simple animals that live in the sea.

brood
A family of young animals produced in one hatching or birth.

camouflage
Shapes and colours that help an animal to blend in with its background, so that it can hide from its enemies.

carnivorous
Describes a flesh-eating animal, especially one from the Carnivora order, which includes dogs, cats and bears.

carrion
The flesh of a dead animal.

cells
The microscopic packages from which all living things are made.

cold-blooded
Describes an animal that cannot control its own body temperature, which changes according to the surroundings.

echolocation
The way that some animals, such as bats, find their way and locate prey by making sounds and using the returned echoes to work out their surroundings.

evolution
Gradual changing of animal species through time.

extinct
Describes an animal or plant that has died out globally, never to reappear.

fossil
Remains of living things that have been preserved in the ground. In most fossils, the original remains are replaced by hard minerals, which can keep their shape for millions of years.

gill
An organ used by aquatic animals to extract oxygen from water.

gland
A group of cells or an organ in the body that produces a particular substance, such as poison.

herbivore
An animal that feeds on plants.

hibernation
A period of sleeping during winter. During hibernation, an animal's bodily functions slow down.

incisors
A mammal's sharp-edged front teeth, used for scraping meat from bones or cutting vegetable matter.

incubation
In birds, the period when a parent sits on the eggs and warms them so that they can develop before hatching.

invertebrate
An animal that does not have a backbone.

larva (plural: larvae)
The second stage in the life of an insect, between the egg and the adult.

ligament
Tough, fibrous tissue that connects muscle to bone.

mammal
An animal that gives birth to live young, which feed on mother's milk. Lions and bears are mammals.

metabolism
The chemical processes that take place in an animal's body. Some of these processes break down food to release energy. Others use energy, for example by making muscles move.

migration
A journey to a different region of the world, usually in the same season each year. Animals migrate so that they can find good breeding conditions in one place, and good wintering conditions in another.

mimic
An animal that copies another, often in order to avoid being eaten.

moult
The shedding of fur, feather or skin so that the body can replace it.

nocturnal
Describes an animal that is active mainly at night and sleeps during the day.

nutrient
Something that provides nourishment for life and growth.

organ
A structure inside the body that carries out different tasks.

paralysis
A state in which the body, or part of the body, loses the ability to move or feel. Venom can cause paralysis and, in some cases, death.

parasite
An animal that lives or feeds on or inside another living animal.

plankton
Floating microscopic organisms that drift in open water. They are a vital source of food for many marine animals.

predator
An animal that hunts and kills other animals.

prehistoric
Something that existed before recorded history began.

prey
Animals that are hunted by others as food. Plant-eating dinosaurs were prey animals, but so were many predatory dinosaurs, because they were hunted by dinosaurs larger than themselves.

proboscis
A long, flexible snout.

pupa (plural: pupae)
The resting, non-feeding stage during the life cycle of an insect when it transforms from a larva into an adult.

quills
Long, sharp spines that grow from the body of a porcupine.

rainforest
A thick forest, with very tall trees, that grows in tropical countries where it is hot all year round and rains every day.

reptile
A cold-blooded animal with scaly skin, for example a snake. Some reptiles lay eggs and others give birth to live young.

saliva
Liquid produced in the mouth to make food easier to swallow.

scavenger
An animal that feeds on carrion.

silk
A fibrous material made by spiders and some insects. Silk is liquid when it is squeezed out of the body but turns into an elastic fibre when stretched and exposed to air.

stoop
To swoop down, for example a hawk diving down to catch a rabbit.

subtropical
Found in the subtropics – the warm region between the hot tropics closer to the Equator, and the cooler, temperate parts of the world.

talons
The sharp claws of birds of prey that they use to snatch up their quarry.

thorax
In animals such as insects, the middle part of the body, found between the head and abdomen.

toxin
A poisonous substance, especially one formed in the body.

tropical
Found in the tropics – the hot parts of the world on either side of the Equator.

tundra
A vast treeless region of northern Europe, Asia and North America where the subsoil is frozen all year.

venom
The poisonous fluid that some animals, such as snakes, inject into their prey.

vertebra (plural: vertebrae)
Bones that link together to form the backbone, or spine, of an animal.

vertebrate
An animal that has a backbone.

INDEX

JK

Jacobson's organ 38, 41
jellyfish 7
jerboas 24
kingfishers 35, 36
Komodo dragons 8, 50, 51

L

larvae 7, 58, 70
leopard frogs 49
leopards 12–13, 26
lions 12, 14, 20–21
living fossils 39, 63
lizards 38, 41, 46, 50–51, 54
lobsters 68–69
locusts 68–69
lyrebirds 28

M

mallee fowl 30
mammals 7, 9–26
manta rays 58–59
marine toads *see* cane toads
mating 18, 28, 29
mice 16
migration 22, 23, 68–69
milksnakes 46
molluscs 7
monarch butterflies 69
monitor lizards 50
monkeys 15
monotremes 7
moose 18–19
moulting 25, 55
musk oxen 14, 23

N

nests 30–31, 32, 33, 73
Nile crocodiles 52, 53

O

omnivores 10
orchid mantises 70
ospreys 34–35
ostriches 32, 33, 36
otters 26
owls 6, 34

P

pack hunting 14, 15, 18–19
pangolins 15, 20, 21
panther chameleons 47
parasites 70
parrots 35
peacocks 28
pelicans 35
penguins 28, 32
peregrines 34
photophores 62
phytoplankton 69
piranhas 64–65
playing dead 47, 49
poison (venom, toxins) 40, 41, 44, 45, 48, 49, 50, 51, 55, 70, 74, 75
poison-dart frogs 44, 45, 49
porcupines 20–21
praying mantises 70, 76
prehistoric animals 21
puffins 31
pythons 42

R

rats 48, 51
rattlesnakes 40–41
rays 58–59
red colobus monkeys 15
red kites 28
reptiles 6, 38–43, 46–47, 50–55, 56
robber flies 70, 73
rock scorpions 74
rodents 16–17, 25
ruminants 13

S

salamanders 48
saltwater crocodiles 52
scavengers 10, 12, 34, 51
scorpions 74–75, 76
sea snakes 40, 65
seahorses 58, 59
sharks 58, 61, 63
shells 6, 7, 46
shrews 10, 11
skunks 21
sloths 14
snakes 38–43, 45, 46, 48, 54, 55
song 28
spiders 8, 45, 70, 71, 76

spiny lobsters 68–69

spiny lobsters 68–69
squirrels 16, 24
starfish 60
stings 72, 73, 74, 75
storks 30, 34
Surinam toads 49
swallows 31
swim bladder 58, 59

T

tail shedding 46
tanagers 36
tarantulas 45
teeth 16, 52, 53, 64
termites 10, 11
thorny devils 46
tiger snakes 55
tigers 8, 14
toads 44–45, 48–49, 56
tortoises 46, 54
tragopans 28
trapdoor spiders 71
tree frogs 7
tripodfish 63
tuataras 39
turkeys 28
turtles 6, 39, 42, 46, 54, 66

V

vertebrates 6, 7
vicuñas 24
vipers 38–39
voles 16
vultures 34

W

warblers 32
warm-blooded animals 6
warning coloration 45, 46, 49, 51
wasps 70
weaver birds 30, 31
whales 11, 13
wildebeest 22–23
wolves 14, 18–19, 23, 26
woodpeckers 28, 30
wrens 28

Z

zebras 14, 26, 53
zooplankton 69